Jennifer Adam

Balisong

T0273388

Salamander Street

PLAYS

First published in 2021 by Salamander Street Ltd.
(info@salamanderstreet.com)

Balisong © Jennifer Adam, 2021

All rights reserved.

Application for professional and amateur performance rights should be
directed to the author c/o Salamander Street. No performance may be given
unless a licence has been obtained, and no alterations may be made in the
title or the text of the adaptation without the author's prior written consent.

You may not copy, store, distribute, transmit, reproduce or otherwise make
available this publication (or any part of it) in any form, or binding or by any
means (print, electronic, digital, optical, mechanical, photocopying, recording
or otherwise), without the prior written permission of the publisher. Any
person who does any unauthorized act in relation to this publication may be
liable to criminal prosecution and civil claims for damages.

ISBN: 9781914228377

10 9 8 7 6 5 4 3 2 1

Characters

AARON RYAN, 16, Scottish

EVIE ROWE, 15, Scottish

RACHEL REYNOLDS, 16 Scottish

Note: Dialogue in italics is said by someone other than Aaron, Evie and Rachel and this should be made clear in the actor's performance

The *Balisong* schools theatre tour was commissioned by No Knives Better Lives (NKBL) as part of their ongoing bystander approach to knife crime in Scotland.

The play was produced by Fast Forward in collaboration with Strange Town. The tour ran for three consecutive years with three different casts, delivering 225 performances to an audience of over 44,000 young people.

The first performance of *Balisong* took place on 25th September 2017 at Boroughmuir High School. The casts were as follows:

CAST ONE – 2017

EVIE: Ashleigh More

RACHEL: Madeline Crabb

AARON: Daniel McGuire

CAST TWO – 2018/19

EVIE: Kirsty Pickering

RACHEL: Suzanne O'Brien

AARON: Fraser MacRae

CAST THREE – 2019

EVIE: Suzanne O'Brien

RACHEL: Rebecca Forsyth

AARON: Joel Anderson

PRODUCER AND TOUR MANAGER/CO-ORDINATOR/FACILITATOR:
    Kai Peacock – Arts Project Director, Fast Forward

DIRECTOR: Steve Small – Creative Director, Strange Town

STAGE MANAGERS: Annie Winton 2017, Danielle El Jorr 2018 & Lottie Avery 2019

www.fastforward.org.uk

www.strangetown.org.uk

www.noknivesbetterlives.com

A stage with four chairs. One of them is empty.

AARON: Finlay Richards.

EVIE: Ritchie.

RACHEL: Everyone knows that name.

EVIE: One of seven kids.

AARON: The Ritchie family.

RACHEL: Everyone knows someone

AARON: One of them

EVIE: The sister that got the dux two years in a row

RACHEL: The eldest brother that did that cycling thing for charity

AARON: The dad that used to play for Hearts

RACHEL: The mum that works for the Government…or something mental like that.

AARON: Everyone knows the Ritchies

EVIE: Everyone knows that name.

RACHEL: Finlay Richards.

EVIE: Finn.

AARON: Known him since Primary School

EVIE: Since nursery

AARON: Since forever

RACHEL: Known as Ritchie mostly

Because of his surname

EVIE: Because his big brothers and big sisters were also known as 'Ritchie'

RACHEL: That's just how it works

AARON: You call the house and ask for Ritchie, and you never know who you'll get on the phone.

EVIE: Finn – Our Ritchie – is the second youngest in a family of nine.

RACHEL: Nine including the parents.

AARON: Farrah – baby Ritchie – she was last.

EVIE: She was last by four minutes.

AARON: Finn's twin.

RACHEL: Finn likes to emphasise those four minutes.

AARON: They were important.

EVIE: Those four minutes kept Finn from being the child.

AARON: From being the baby.

EVIE: He's the second shortest in the entire family,

RACHEL: Second only to his eighty-nine-year-old granny. And she hunches.

EVIE: Even Farrah was a quarter of an inch taller.

AARON: The pencil marks on the door frame

EVIE: Ages and heights

RACHEL: A constant reminder.

EVIE: But what he lacks in height, he makes up for in originality.

AARON: In humour.

RACHEL: Or at least,

in sheer weirdness.

AARON: When he was wee, Finn asked for a magic kit for his birthday.

EVIE: While his brothers and sisters played with Lego or cars or board games

RACHEL: Finn had scarves,

A wand, deck of cards.

EVIE: He loved being the only one

AARON: Having the control

EVIE: He loved knowing all the secrets

RACHEL: Stuffing coins up his sleeves

AARON: Hiding behind sofas and pretending to be invisible

RACHEL: I remember him wearing a top hat and cape to school for a fortnight.

EVIE: Showing off.

AARON: Standing out.

RACHEL: All eyes on Finn.

EVIE: Until a teacher pulled him up for not wearing a tie

AARON: Didn't care so much about the outfit,

EVIE: But no tie means a punishment exercise.

RACHEL: Finn told her not to bother.

He'd just make it disappear.

AARON: Five minutes later he's in the Rector's office

Getting told off for being a total wideo.

RACHEL: And it's not just at school

It's on holiday,

EVIE: days out

AARON: Even family weddings

RACHEL: Every photograph in the Ritchie house,

EVIE: Every image of that family

RACHEL: Ritchie after Ritchie

AARON: In smart suits or dresses

EVIE: In shorts and T-shirts

RACHEL: Swimwear

AARON: Sportswear

EVIE: You knew they were a family,

RACHEL: You knew they were all one, by the way they dressed

AARON: By the way they looked

EVIE: Except,

    right in the middle,

RACHEL: The centre of every picture

AARON: Your eyes are drawn

    To Finn

EVIE: Wearing bright yellow

RACHEL: and green

AARON: and pink

EVIE: A multi-coloured neon jacket that you could spot in a sandstorm

RACHEL: Something that should have died along with the 90s

AARON: Left around the house after a decade of hand me downs

EVIE: And now there it was, wrapped around Finn, like armour,

    in every photograph

RACHEL: Even in the height of summer

    Thin baggy sleeves,

EVIE: The colour stretching right to his fingertips

AARON: So when he waved,

    It made him look like he had wings.

EVIE: Multicoloured, neon wings.

Pause.

AARON: At least,

   We knew we'd never lose him.

RACHEL: I suppose he likes to stand out.

AARON: I suppose he likes to be loud.

   To shout.

EVIE: Even if there are an awful lot of people to shout over.

RACHEL: Ever noticed how it's the shortest kids that make the most noise?

EVIE: Imagine how much noise you'd have to make in this house

AARON: The Ritchie house

EVIE: Every room, filled with people – as standard.

RACHEL: Aunties and uncles and grannies

   and nieces and nephews and babies and neighbours

AARON: Kinda like our houses at Christmas.

EVIE: That's what it was like every day in the Ritchie house.

RACHEL: You'd go round for dinner,

   Parents would cook something nice

AARON: Masses of food

RACHEL: And yet all *I* ever seemed to get was salad.

AARON: Cos if you didn't eat fast, you didn't eat.

EVIE: You'd just sit there opposite nine bobbed heads

   Buried in their pasta bolognese

RACHEL: Inhaling bits of meat

   Sooking the spaghetti and slurping orange Fanta

EVIE: Fighting over the last bit of burnt garlic bread.

AARON: The house is emptier now

They breathe a sigh of relief.

EVIE: All Finn's brothers and sisters went to uni

AARON: Herriot Watt. Strathclyde. Stirling. Abertay. Aberdeen

RACHEL: In that order.

EVIE: One kid in every University city.

RACHEL: All they needed was Finn or Farrah to attend St Andrews

and they'd won University bingo

AARON: Finn isn't interested in University.

RACHEL: Finn wants to travel the world.

EVIE: Couch surf

RACHEL: And live on beaches.

AARON: And he doesn't fancy the likes of Portobello Beach.

Or the silver sands of Aberdour.

EVIE: Finn wants away.

RACHEL: Away, away.

AARON: Australia. Or Bali. Or Thailand.

EVIE: But Finn is fifteen.

So this year, Finn would have to settle for the Netherlands.

2.

AARON: Seven hours in the coach from Fife to Hull.

RACHEL: Felt like seven weeks.

AARON: Overnight in the boat to Rotterdam

EVIE: Tiny cabins.

RACHEL: Sea sickness.

AAROB: Back on the coach

RACHEL: Ugh!

AARON: Another hour to Amsterdam

EVIE: For flower markets

RACHEL: I'm allergic.

AARON: Cheese factory

RACHEL: I'm allergic.

EVIE: Windmill visit?

RACHEL: *(Sighs.)* …Fine.

AARON: Then forty-five minutes of free time

EVIE: *Don't wander off on your own!*

RACHEL: They try to make you feel like you've earned it,

EVIE: Like you're an adult who can be trusted by yourself

RACHEL: But really, the teachers just want a bloody break.

AARON: Fine by us,

RACHEL: So we're off

   Literally running away, looking for cafes, shops,

AARON: Time to buy souvenirs and that

EVIE: Postcards that would arrive home a week after we did.

EVIE: They have china swans

RACHEL: The kind of thing your granny has on her mantlepiece

AARON: Clogs! Real clogs that you could wear and everything!

RACHEL: Chocolates with alcohol in them!

EVIE: *So* much chocolate!

AARON: but something else had caught Finn's eye

They turn to look at **FINN**.

AARON: He's on the other side of the street, standing in front of this man selling gadgets

RACHEL: Torches and lighters and pipes

AARON: We run over to him

and he's mesmerized by this gadget guy

EVIE: The way he's moving

RACHEL: The way he holds…

Whatever he's holding in his hands

AARON: And Finn's watching this guy

EVIE: watching his arms snaking,

RACHEL: His fingers rolling and catching and flicking

EVIE: Finn's eyes fixated on the motion.

AARON: The guy is so good, he hardly needs to concentrate.

EVIE: He barely blinks.

RACHEL: Then he spots Finn, he smiles and he says,

AARON: "*feef-teen*"

RACHEL: And Finn looks up at him, finally taking his eyes away from the guy's hands

AARON: "*Feef-teen Euros,*"

RACHEL: the guy says again.

EVIE: Bargain!

RACHEL: I don't know what it is, but I love it,

AARON: It's cool as fuck!

EVIE: You could learn the tricks!

AARON: Do all that magic stuff!

RACHEL: I defo want a shot

AARON: We could show folk on the boat on the way home!

EVIE: Finn pulls out a twenty

AAROB: The gadget guys says he hasn't got any change,

RACHEL: Finn doesn't care, he hands over the note,

EVIE: Grabs the box

AARON: The shiny sleeve protecting it from inexperienced hands

RACHEL: We all look at it

AARON: Stuffed in its packaging.

RACHEL: Balisong.

AARON: Tripple Flick XL

Pause.

RACHEL: Get it out then!

EVIE: Finn rips the cardboard apart, tearing at the plastic

It stiffens and goes that foggy way

AARON: And the four of us yank at it to get it out

RACHEL: And it falls onto the ground

But Finn is on it like a dart

EVIE: He holds it in both palms and it stretches from one side to the other

AARON: The knife

expands, arms out

EVIE: Like it's a welcome

RACHEL: Like it's an offering.

Pause.

RACHEL: Show us a trick then!

AARON: Do what that guy was doing!

RACHEL: Spin it about!

EVIE: Finn tries to fold the knife back together,

grasps the handle in a fist and shakes the loose end

They jump back.

AARON: A blade flashes, twice the length of the handle

RACHEL: And he's trying to flick it, like the gadget guy

EVIE: But it just swings round and slices a chunk out of Finn's hand.

AARON: That loose skin between his thumb and finger,

EVIE: Stinging, seeping,

AARON: We looked at Finn.

RACHEL: …You're a total fanny.

AARON: Why would you buy a knife anyway?

EVIE: You'll never get that back on the boat

AARON: What a waste of money

RACHEL: It's a bit pathetic like

AARON: Your dad'll go completely mental

EVIE: You cannae even use it properly.

AARON: You're not on TV mate.

RACHEL: You're not in a gang mate.

EVIE: Can't believe you actually bought a knife.

RACHEL: Total. Fanny.

EVIE: The boat home was another of those overnight jobs

AARON: Two bunk beds in a room the size of a toilet.

EVIE: Teachers roaming the corridor,

RACHEL: poking their pointy noses into every cabin on the way past

AARON: We'd stolen plasters from the trolly in the hall

Trying to stick Finn's hand back together

RACHEL: The stuffing inside the pillows worked a treat

AARON: A thick gauze to catch the blood.

EVIE: *Lights out in ten!*

RACHEL: But there's still folk walking about

Folk laughing and singing from their bunks

EVIE: We were going into bed,

Climbing up the metal ladders when,

They all step back.

AARON: Gary walks in

RACHEL: He offers us some sweeties

EVIE: Crisps and chocolates and fizzy juice from a broken vending machine

AARON: And he looks behind, checks no one watching,

EVIE: Then he pulls out cigarettes and offers us one of those too.

RACHEL: I take one.

AARON: I take the Irn Bru and a Mars bar.

EVIE: Packet of Quavers.

RACHEL: And then he leaves.

AARON: He goes round all of **us**, then he leaves.

EVIE: And Finn's standing there empty handed.

AARON: In plain sight

RACHEL: Shorter, granted.

EVIE: But right there.

AARON: Right next to us.

Awkward silence.

EVIE: Probably heard the teachers' coming back

AARON: Probably off to get more

RACHEL: Probably didn't want to touch Finn's manky hand.

EVIE: Finn is glowing.

His bright pink skin.

AARON: Flushed cheeks.

RACHEL: And he stands there,

This bizarre beacon

EVIE: Otherwise camouflaged next to the beige-coloured cabin

AARON: Gary Rose

EVIE: Not quite as delicate in nature as his name would suggest

RACHEL: Gary is sixteen. He is almost six feet tall.

AARON: Gary is not like Finn.

RACHEL: Gary did not ever

wear a top hat and cape to school. ***Ever***.

EVIE: Gary does not notice

that he has completely ignored the fourth person in the room.

AARON: Like he didn't even matter,

EVIE: Like he was invisible.

AARON: So it's not odd behaviour,

EVIE: Not odd at all that a month later, when Gary invites us round.

RACHEL: Us and half the school

EVIE: Us three, *and* Finn.

AARON: Invites us round to his house for party.

EVIE: It's not odd

    that Finn is nervous,

RACHEL: suspicious

AARON: Because in Finn's head, that's a month of radio silence

EVIE: That's four weeks of invisibility.

RACHEL: Following on from eleven years of invisibility.

EVIE: So perhaps it's not surprising,

AARON: Maybe it's really obvious

RACHEL: Makes sense

EVIE: That Finn is ready to be seen.

3.

AARON: So we're sitting in Gary's house.

RACHEL: An actual mansion in the next village.

EVIE: Six bedrooms.

AARON: Two living rooms.

RACHEL: Four bathrooms.

EVIE: I counted five.

RACHEL: Every inch, wallpapered and upholstered

    so that you couldn't see a single join

AARON: Not one crack.

EVIE: Gary's parents are on holiday.

Obviously.

RACHEL: And it's almost ten o'clock

AARON: It's almost too late,

EVIE: But having not spoken to him all night,

RACHEL: Not so much as a 'Hey'

AARON: Gary hands Finn a £20 note and tells him to pick up a bottle

RACHEL: Vodka. Rum. Whatever's cheapest.

EVIE: Now. Before the shop shuts.

RACHEL: And he goes.

EVIE: Finn takes the money and he leaves.

AARON: And I go with him because it's clear he doesn't want to

EVIE: And it's clear *why* he doesn't want to

RACHEL: But they leave with twelve minutes to spare,

AARON: But we make it,

RACHEL: They make it just in time,

AARON: And the shopkeeper knows exactly why we're here.

We linger around the wine as if we're considering an after-dinner port

EVIE: And we're back here listening to Gary,

RACHEL: *'I better get ma twenty quid back when he doesnae get served'*

AARON: Finn goes to grab a bottle of vodka, but I get there first.

I look older, so I take it up to the cashier.

RACHEL: *'They're no coming back with that bottle.'*

AARON: The guy looks at me.

Then glares at Finn, who's pretending to rummage through the ten p crisp packets

And he asks,

'And has your pal got ID?'

RACHEL: He didn't really want the booze.

EVIE: If he did he'd have gone himself.

RACHEL: Or got Big Stevie to go.

EVIE: Big Stevie hasn't been ID'd since he was nine.

RACHEL: So when they returned, empty handed

EVIE: Empty except for two packets of Skips they'd bought with Gary's money

RACHEL: Gary made sure everybody knew about it.

AARON: Takes pictures of the two of us,

RACHEL: Finn stuffing his face to avoid trying to explain

AARON: Pictures that are on Facebook within thirty seconds

EVIE: Liked and shared by everyone who was there

RACHEL: And everyone who wasn't there

EVIE: It was like wildfire

Spreading from wall to wall

AARON: I didn't care. If anything, I had proof that I ***didn't*** illegally buy alcohol.

RACHEL: Finn went quiet,

EVIE: Faded almost

AARON: He was smiling

RACHEL: Trying to be part of the joke

AARON: to laugh along

EVIE: Trying to shift the focus.

RACHEL: Then he bolts.

AARON: disappears upstairs

EVIE: But the laughing echoes through the house

    Ringing through each decorated wall

RACHEL: But it's cut short,

AARON: It's interrupted by gasps

RACHEL: In comes Finn,

AARON: He returns without a word,

EVIE: Everyone looking at him now,

RACHEL: Many genuinely interested,

    In a half-pissed sort of way

AARON: He'd been practising, that was obvious

EVIE: And when Finn walks in waving the butterfly knife around

AARON: Twirling it between his fingers

EVIE: And flicking it across his wrists

RACHEL: Everyone stops. Everyone watches.

EVIE: It's like someone playing with fire,

    You know it's dangerous, but you want to watch anyway

RACHEL: You want to see, what might happen

AARON: What could happen.

EVIE: And I can't take my eyes off the scars

RACHEL: The crimson red scratches on his hands

AARON: The pitfalls of practice

EVIE: Yellow and purple bruises across his skin

RACHEL: Just a glimpse

EVIE: The colours flashing as he moves

AARON: And the sound of his arms moving against his body

RACHEL: Rubbing the material, scuffing the sides

AARON: It's like a bird

EVIE: Like wings flapping

RACHEL: Trapped

AARON: Trying to escape

EVIE: And we watch Finn

RACHEL: And we listen

AARON: And it's all quite hypnotic actually

EVIE: We are all

Taken in

AARON: until,

RACHEL: *'You carry a knife, mate'*

AARON: Gary cuts through the silence

They all turn and look at **GARY**.

RACHEL: *'You get stabbed.'*

Pause, the mood changes.

EVIE: Was that a threat?

RACHEL: Is that a fact?

EVIE: Did Gary just threaten Finn?

AARON: Finn catches the knife. He holds it tight in his palm.

EVIE: I go to him

And I have to prise it out his fingers

I hold it like it's diseased

Use my sleeve to put it inside Finn's backpack.

AARON: They take a moment

RACHEL: They stare at Finn,

AARON: The sweat resting on his brow and upper lip

Pause.

RACHEL: And then they go back to drinking.

AARON: Singing to the music.

EVIE: Like nothing had happened.

RACHEL: Like nobody cared.

AARON: And Finn smiles.

Because he had them,

EVIE: Just for a moment, he had them all.

4.

RACHEL: And that's how it started.

EVIE: A performance of sorts

RACHEL: An art form

AARON: To look cool

EVIE: To entertain

AARON: Show off

RACHEL: Stand out

EVIE: Something different,

RACHEL: And it works

It totally works

AARON: And so Finn would watch YouTube videos

RACHEL: Google how they were made

AARON: So that he understood,

EVIE: Understood the art of the balisong.

AARON: We try to watch with him

RACHEL: Try to understand the fascination

EVIE: The obsession

AARON: And so we sit in his bedroom

RACHEL: We watch American men play with knives on the internet

EVIE: For entertainment

RACHEL: Performing all the tricks we've seen Finn do

EVIE: He shows us one of Angelina Jolie

RACHEL: On a chat show couch

AARON: Flicking, spinning, twisting…

EVIE: And then it spills into another video

RACHEL: Another American

AARON: A knife shaped like a claw

EVIE: The guy on the video wraps beef in clingfilm,

A plastic bag, then a t-shirt

RACHEL: And we watch as he swings his fist past the lump of meat,

AARON: Hanging, tied to the ceiling

EVIE: Expressionless, one swift movement

RACHEL: And we listen as his blade slices through clothing,

ARRON: Skin

RACHEL: Muscle

EVIE: And bone.

RACHEL: *'That is a thing of beauty'*

EVIE: the guy says. Inspecting the wound

AARON: A caution flashes up on the screen,

EVIE: *'No meat was wasted in the making of this video'*

RACHEL: Aye. Because food waste is what I'm concerned about right now…

EVIE: I'm no veggie. But I'm starting to feel sick

RACHEL: Why do these things even exist?

EVIE: This is super unhygienic.

AARON: But for Finn,

It makes it more appealing.

Because in some weird way,

People want to be disgusted

EVIE: Like it makes them tough for being able to watch

RACHEL: For being able to stomach it

EVIE: I tell Finn, 'You need to chuck that thing'

RACHEL: But he gets angry

AARON: Yeh, I know we wanted you to buy it

RACHEL: I know it looked cool in Amsterdam

AARON: C'mon mate. Just get rid.

EVIE: And he thinks about it.

I'm sure he thinks about it.

AARON: But he says nothing.

EVIE: Just sort of pouts a bit

AARON: Like he's hurt

RACHEL: Like he's a kid.

EVIE: The kid with the butterfly knife

AARON: Finn doesn't throw away his knife.

RACHEL: Finn decides, he'll keep it for now.

EVIE: Finn folds it together and places it back into his pocket

Securing it between the material.

AARON: And you think,

RACHEL: You know

EVIE: We should tell someone

AARON: But we can't tell Finn's dad, he'd go mental.

RACHEL: And we can't tell our parents because they'd tell Finn's parents

EVIE: And we can't tell a teacher because, we're not seven years old.

RACHEL: Snitches get stitches.

AARON: And we're not going to grass him up

EVIE: Of course we're not

AARON: Finn isn't dangerous

EVIE: But he's still carrying a knife

RACHEL: If there was someone

Anyone

AARON: If there was one person we could speak to…

EVIE: Farrah.

(To the others.) …We could tell Farrah?

5.

RACHEL: It's a while before we see Finn again

AARON: You're talking weeks, months even

RACHEL: See him properly anyway

EVIE: He'd be in class,

RACHEL: Hanging about by the bike sheds at break

AARON: We see him in the canteen

EVIE: Packed lunch he's made himself,

AARON: Last night's leftovers

RACHEL: Finally there's leftovers

AARON: Because there's nobody there now

EVIE: Hardly anybody left in that house.

RACHEL: We'd see him walking into school

AARON: And we'd see him leave.

EVIE: So we *do* see him,

RACHEL: It's not like he completely disappears,

AARON: He just had,

Others.

EVIE: He'd meet other folk at the school gates

AARON: Ex pupils that had already left school

RACHEL: The ones that were super keen to get out the minute they hit sixteen

AARON: now always there

RACHEL: Always hanging about

EVIE: 3.30 every day

AARON: Like they're desperate to get back in

RACHEL: Like they're afraid of missing something

AARON: Those guys

RACHEL: They were Finn's friends now.

EVIE: They liked Finn.

RACHEL: They liked Finn's knife.

Pause.

AARON: And it's not long

EVIE: Pretty soon

RACHEL: We only *hear* about Finn.

EVIE: Word gets round

AARON: Only rumours like

RACHEL: That Finn was hanging around outside the Spar,

Offering a cheeky flash at his new toy

AARON: That didn't happen.

RACHEL: Asking someone to buy him alcohol.

AARON: *(To* **RACHEL**.*)* It didn't happen.

EVIE: Someone else said he had it at the park.

RACHEL: Showing it off, doing tricks,

EVIE: offering it out, letting people touch it

Run their fingers along the blade

AARON: I just find it difficult to believe –

RACHEL: But, he hangs out with those guys now

AARON: So there's a part of you that thinks…

RACHEL: And there's a part of you that knows,

EVIE: …This needs to be addressed.

AARON: So we go to his house

EVIE: All three of us.

   So he knows we're serious

RACHEL: Stride up his driveway

AARON: Chap at his door.

EVIE: …And Farrah opens it

   EVIE'S *eyes widen. She wants to speak to* **FARRAH**.

AARON: Like she was waiting for us to knock

RACHEL: Like she knew what we were about to say

EVIE: Like she knew it was her we wanted to see, not Finn.

RACHEL: And for a second she waits,

AARON: And we look at Evie

RACHEL: *(To* **EVIE**.*)* C'mon then!

AARON: And she goes to speak

EVIE: And for a second,

   I hesitate –

   I hesitate because,

   There's these images

   Flooding my head

   Not of the Spar park at night

   Not of clothed meat being sliced in a basement

   Not Angelina Jolie

   Not the bruises and cuts on Finn's arms.

   It's the cape.

It's the wand. The scarves.

It's Finn suddenly six feet tall.

And constantly smiling

It's the guy that doesn't really need to wear the neon jacket anymore.

And it's not that I think it's okay,

It's just that I hesitate,

And then –

RACHEL: And then, she's gone

They watch **FARRAH** *walk away from them.*

AARON: On her way out,

EVIE: And I go to shout her name but,

AARON: She darts down the driveway

And slips inside a Skoda Fabia

RACHEL: Pounding from in the inside out.

AARON: It drives off and we're left

EVIE: Left in a cloud of exhaust smoke

RACHEL: Her front door lying open

and moving with the draft

Pause.

AARON: Only one thing for it.

EVIE: So we go in

AARON: We climb the stairs and find Finn in his bedroom

RACHEL: Glued to the computer

AARON: He looks up at us when we come in

Throws an upward nod in our direction

EVIE: Like it was no big deal.

RACHEL: Like he hadn't just dingyed us for the last month.

AARON: He shuts the face of the laptop,

Folds it with a snap

RACHEL: And he looks at us

EVIE: His eyes glaze over

AARON: Maybe from the darkness of the room

EVIE: The lack of actual sunlight

RACHEL: Maybe strained from watching hours of YouTube videos

AARON: Of Googling and searching and learning

EVIE: We had talked about being rational.

RACHEL: If we were going to speak directly to Finn,

kindness would be better than concern.

AARON: We'll be totally fair

RACHEL: Finn was our pal

EVIE: We had to be calm.

They are anything but calm.

EVIE: Where have you been?!

AARON: Why are you hanging out with **them**?

RACHEL: Were you at the park last night?

AARON: What were you doing?

EVIE: What are you thinking?

AARON: Does your dad know?

EVIE: It'll get you in trouble

RACHEL: You need to get rid of that thing

EVIE: before it gets *you* in trouble.

AARON: But he's out.

RACHEL: He's either not listening or not interested.

EVIE: I walk over to him

    I hold him in place. Fuse my hands to his shoulders

    I look at him. Wait for him to meet my eyes.

    And I say, 'Tell me.'

RACHEL: Just a blank stare

EVIE: I move my hand into his trouser pocket.

    He flinches.

    Tries to back away but when he does,

    It's in my hand.

    And I hold it, flat on my palm.

AARON: Finn snatches the knife from Evie's hand.

EVIE: Gives me this look as if I'd just tried to swipe his wallet.

    So we make him promise,

RACHEL: If he won't bin it,

    lock it up in a drawer.

AARON: Leave it at home. Hidden away.

EVIE: And he thinks about it.

    I'm sure he thinks about it.

AARON: But he says nothing.

RACHEL: He says nothing because by this time,

    Finn thinks it's magic.

AARON: Finn thinks it has power.

RACHEL: And maybe he's right.

*They move away to signify them leaving **FINN'S** room.*

Because it gets to a point where other people are attracted to it

AARON: Heard about Finn's blade from a pal or a cousin

EVIE: Heard about his tricks

RACHEL: The mesmerizing movement

AARON: So perhaps it's not surprising,

That someone else might try to steal it

EVIE: Take it away from Finn

RACHEL: What's stupid however

AARON: What Finn could have told you, because he learned it on
day one

EVIE: Lesson one,

RACHEL: You don't try to swipe a butterfly knife whilst it's in motion,

Dancing in someone else's hands

AARON: We hear it directly

EVIE: From some 6th year that saw it all

RACHEL: Finn saw him – a stranger really – a guy from another town

AARON: He moved towards Finn, the guy's eyes fixed on the shiny
sharp edge

Like a magpie, watching it gleam

AARON: He wanted it.

RACHEL: he wanted that knife.

AARON: Finn saw it coming

EVIE: he grabbed the handle tight

AARON: and bam! –

RACHEL: Finn stepped forward,

    The blade inches from the man's face

AARON: It does that

RACHEL: I've seen it

EVIE: It's *that* fast

RACHEL: One swift jab and...

AARON: The guy blinked, his eyes filled with water

EVIE: With relief

AARON: He stepped back from Finn and he walked away.

RACHEL: The guy actually walked away from him.

AARON: Finn stuffs the knife into his pocket.

EVIE: Hidden.

AARON: And everyone turned to look at Finn

RACHEL: To look at him in awe.

AARON: And it's from that moment

RACHEL: That evening

EVIE: That we knew

AARON: For reasons of status,

RACHEL: Or power,

EVIE: Or protection,

AARON: we knew

EVIE: That knife would never leave Finn's jacket pocket.

6.

AARON *steps up. Separates himself from* **EVIE** *and* **RACHEL**.

AARON: There's this computer game.

Zombie Nation.

Brand new.

Been advertised for months,

And now it had been released,

And we'd said,

Finn and I,

We said we'd complete it together.

First.

Before anyone else.

Seemed like the perfect excuse to speak to him.

The perfect reason to get him round.

AARON *sits on a chair next to another empty one just like it. He mimics playing a computer game.*

It's tricky at first, you have to avoid being caught.

Avoid the transformation from living, to dead, to undead.

We're both totally shit at it.

We go through eighteen lives in forty-five minutes.

But after a while, I start to get it.

And I survive for about an hour. Hour and a half tops.

Then they find me.

But I'm better than Finn. He gets caught after twenty minutes.

Every time, just when he's getting going.

And I'm starting to think he's doing it deliberately.

Like he loses interest.

So I think about suggesting a different game,

But I really, *really* want to complete this.

It's become a personal vendetta.

I need to beat it.

So, I watch him play.

Starting and stopping and starting again.

Never really getting further than the first stage without becoming a zombie.

And then it occurs to me one evening,

We're playing,

Finn's turn.

And in under five minutes this time, Finn's dead.

Then undead. Then he keeps playing.

They let you do that. You don't score points,

but they let you continue, if you want.

It's easier I suppose, jumping ship like that.

Switching sides.

It's not the point of the game, you're supposed to defeat them.

You're supposed to be the hero.

But Finn didn't see it like that.

Because when you're the undead, you have an automatic advantage.

An instant weapon.

Fear.

And that's when I see it.

The real power of fear.

Being able to instill that into somebody,

It's like magic.

So I try it.

My go comes round.

I run to the first Zombie I see. Let him rip the skin from my bones.

Feed off my flesh.

It's brutal.

And after that, no one bothers you.

They see you

And then they run.

7.

RACHEL: It's the last day of school.

EVIE: Summer holidays

AARON: Exams over,

For this year anyway,

EVIE: Just get me to one o'clock.

RACHEL: Then it's six weeks of freedom

AARON: Six weeks of friends and parties and sleeping in

RACHEL: It's funny how punctual you are

on the last day of school.

All year we struggle, sleep in

miss the bus,

making the bell in James Bond time

But today, everyone's early

AARON: Everyone makes the effort on the last day

RACHEL: Because let's face it,

Nothing happens on the last day.

EVIE: Streaming films,

AARON: Social media

EVIE: Spotify, selfies,

RACHEL: *That's* what happens on the last day of school.

AARON: No one told Finn.

EVIE: Waltzes into RME at 12.15 entirely unnoticed

RACHEL: Like he's appearing from thin air

AARON: Slips into his seat without the teacher batting an eyelid.

EVIE: He opens his note book and 4…3…2…

The bell rings.

RACHEL: He gets up

Eyeballs the class

AARON: But speaks to nobody

EVIE: And he leaves

AARON: He becomes swept up among the bodies in the corridor.

RACHEL: And he has this look

EVIE: I couldn't be sure.

RACHEL: Like something's different

EVIE: I couldn't be completely certain

AARON: Something's changed

RACHEL: He looks taller

AARON: Walks slower

RACHEL: Makes eye contact

EVIE: Looks at me as if to say,

'Tell me'

RACHEL: He stares me out

EVIE: 'Why didn't you tell me?'

AARON: Then he walks away

EVIE: But I don't know anything for definite.

AARON: I think about following him

EVIE: What if –

AARON: I call his name

RACHEL: But he's off round the corner

EVIE: What if –

AARON: I lose him as he dodges between prefects and first years

RACHEL: Vanishing behind coats and school bags

The bell rings again, they're right next to it, they all shield their ears.

AARON: And he's gone.

EVIE: *(To others.)* What if he's seen that video?

Pause.

EVIE: You see, he'd gone in.

By himself

AARON: Didn't want his dad to know I suppose

RACHEL: Saved up the cash his mum had given him

EVIE: A fiver a month for washing dishes

RACHEL: Shite money

AARON: Even though they had a dish washer,

EVIE: Like, every night,

RACHEL: Scrubbing pots and pans, for this measly fiver

AARON: But he'd saved it up

He had enough to go in and buy it

RACHEL: Zombie Nation

AARON: Wanted his own copy.

EVIE: He picked up the over-eighteens' box

RACHEL: Walked over to the counter,

AARON: Looked up at the guy at the till.

EVIE: Finn was not eighteen.

AARON: Finn did not look eighteen.

RACHEL: Finn looked twelve.

EVIE: Finn was not served that game.

RACHEL: But Gary.

AARON: Gary worked at the store.

RACHEL: Gary watched as his boss took the game out of Finn's hands.

EVIE: Shrugged.

RACHEL: Gave him this look as if to say, 'I'm no really sorry'

AARON: There are bullies at our school.

That's for sure,

RACHEL: But Gary?

AARON: Gary isn't one of them.

RACHEL: Gary's just, a complete tit.

EVIE: Like most teenage boys.

RACHEL: Gary had a video on his phone of Finn walking out the shop

Empty handed.

EVIE: He showed it to everyone.

AARON: Passed it round.

EVIE: Everyone laughed.

RACHEL: *We* laughed.

It was the look on Finn's face

AARON: Almost smiling

RACHEL: Like he was in on the gag

EVIE: Comments on the video

AARON*: Short arse.*

RACHEL*: Effing useless.*

AARON*: No wonder we coudnae trust him tae get booze.*

EVIE*: He cannae even buy a computer game.*

RACHEL*: Fucksake man.*

AARON*: Born baby faced*

EVIE*: And he'll die baby faced*

AARON: He's seen it.

RACHEL: He's definitely seen it.

EVIE: You can tell from the way he looks at Gary

RACHEL: And the way Gary's looking back at him from the edge of the
playing field

AARON: And the bell's gone so everyone is piling out

EVIE: Everyone watching this video,

Pointing at Finn.

AARON: And they laugh

EVIE: And they poke him,

   Like physically, fingers out, actual poking him

RACHEL: Who does that?

AARON: And Gary's hands are inches from Finn's face

RACHEL: Do you know how annoying that is?

EVIE: Would drive anybody crazy

AARON: So Finn slaps him

RACHEL: Slaps Gary's hand right out the way

EVIE: And Gary pushes him back,

AARON: Stands up, presses his weight against Finn

EVIE: And I go to move, I'm about to stop it, about to grab Finn,

RACHEL: It's not worth a fight,

AARON: But Gary's hands rise, they go for Finn's throat

EVIE: But before they make it

RACHEL: Before his fingers have the chance to grab

AARON: To wrap around the skin

EVIE: Finn pulls a hand out of his pocket

RACHEL: And quick as anything

AARON: He punches Gary's fat spongy stomach

EVIE: And instantly, we know

AARON: We immediately see it

RACHEL: But take a moment to register what's just happened

EVIE: As Gary's shirt turns red,

RACHEL: soaking, absorbing the white material

AARON: No tricks

RACHEL: No flicking or twirling or catching or spinning

EVIE: No magic

AARON: And Finn, with blood smeared across his hands,

RACHEL: Drops the knife

EVIE: It falls in slow motion to the ground

RACHEL: It clatters on the concrete

AARON: Kids run screaming,

EVIE: Teachers race towards us,

RACHEL: And we just freeze,

EVIE: We don't react at all.

AARON: Somehow stuck in this leaning forward, arms open position

RACHEL: Not running

AARON: Not helping

EVIE: Just stuck

RACHEL: Gary drops to his knees

EVIE: The look on his face, it's just

ARRON: …Fear.

He was afraid.

RACHEL: And as the crimson red blood trickles down to the ends of Finn's fingers

AARON: His arms twitch

EVIE: The fluorescent yellow, the deep purple

RACHEL: The remains of past bruises

peppered across his skin,

AARON: The opposite of camouflage

EVIE: The vibrant colours announce his presence

RACHEL: Like a tactic,

AARON: *Stay. Away.*

EVIE: Finn looks down and they're green now

    Bright green arms

AARON: And pink

RACHEL: And orange

EVIE: And they change,

    Every inch he moves, they blend

RACHEL: Adapt

AARON: Transform

EVIE: Until everyone around him is gone.

AARON: Frightened off.

RACHEL: And those who witnessed it

EVIE: Those who can't unsee that moment

AARON: Those who can't unhear that sound

RACHEL: Of slicing, squelching

AARON: Of final gasps

RACHEL: We're all that's left.

EVIE: And all I can hear is that video

RACHEL: ***That*** *is a thing of beauty*

AARON: The smell of raw meat

EVIE: And I vomit

    Covering my shoes and my hair

AARON: The teachers that run over

RACHEL: The paramedics that try to revive him

AARON: The police that take Finn away to a small room

RACHEL: His parents

EVIE: Both their parents

AARON: Both their siblings

EVIE: The sister who won the dux two years in a row

RACHEL: The brother who did some cycling thing for charity

AARON: Their friends

EVIE: The community

RACHEL: The school

AARON: The council

EVIE: Government

RACHEL: The country

EVIE: Blood seeps from every single person affected.

AARON: And the police tell us they've called our parents

RACHEL: And they look at us.

AARON: All of us.

EVIE: As if we're one,

AARON: As if all our hands were holding Finn's knife

RACHEL: Because if you know

EVIE: If you know and don't stop it

AARON: Don't say anything

RACHEL: Then you might as well

EVIE: You might as well be the one holding the weapon

AARON: And all of a sudden,

EVIE: The sound of paper tearing

RACHEL: a long, drawn out rip

EVIE: A degree offer

AARON: An apprenticeship

RACHEL: A visa

EVIE: Gone.

RACHEL: The pieces float to the floor like snowflakes

AARON: Like frosting

RACHEL: On the hottest day of the year.

EVIE: Landing at our feet.

RACHEL: And we think of him.

AARON: Gary Rose

EVIE: His face.

RACHEL: His name.

AARON: Everyone knows that name.

RACHEL: Gary Rose was sixteen. He had one brother.

EVIE: Gary Rose studied biology and drama and computing and business

AARON: Because Gary Rose didn't know what he wanted to do when he left school.

He hadn't worked it out yet.

RACHEL: Gary Rose was more interested in playing basketball

EVIE: Learning to cook. Playing computer games.

AARON: Gary Rose took his time coming into this world,

RACHEL: His mum was in labour for over thirty-six hours.

EVIE: But he left it, in just four minutes.

AARON: Four important minutes

EVIE: And soon,

    You won't be able to pass a newsagents, a classroom,

RACHEL: Or pick up a newspaper, log onto Facebook, Twitter, Snapchat,

EVIE: Without seeing it

RACHEL: Without hearing it mouthed.

AARON: Gary Rose.

    No longer a person, but an incident. A statistic.

EVIE: Everyone knows that name.

AARON: Everyone knows it now.

    Long pause.

    They move closer to the audience.

RACHEL: But you don't know that name, do you?

EVIE: I mean,

    Before today.

RACHEL: Before coming here

EVIE: You didn't know that name

AARON: Just another young guy

    From another school

RACHEL: Another town

    That you've probably never heard of.

AARON: And maybe,

RACHEL: Just maybe.

EVIE: You haven't heard of him,

Because today, this

isn't what happened.

They reset, they talk fast as if retelling the story.

RACHEL: The video,

AARON: Finn's helpless face

EVIE: Head down as he runs out the shop

AARON: Embarrassed

RACHEL: Total beamer.

EVIE: And now it was doing the rounds

AARON: Everyone saw it

RACHEL: Farrah saw it.

EVIE: Farrah saw it because I showed her.

Because I was ready.

RACHEL: It was suddenly on Facebook

AARON: On YouTube.

RACHEL: Finn stood there while they laughed,

Delivered pacier this time.

EVIE: And they poke him,

Like physically, fingers out, actual poking him

RACHEL: Who does that?

AARON: Gary's hand inches from Finn's face

RACHEL: Do you know how annoying that is?

EVIE: Would drive anybody crazy

AARON: So Finn slaps him

RACHEL: Slaps Gary's hand right out the way

EVIE: And Gary pushes him back,

AARON: Stands up, presses his weight against Finn

EVIE: And I go to move, I'm about to stop it, about to grab Finn,

RACHEL: It's not worth a fight,

AARON: But Gary's hands rise, they go for Finn's throat

EVIE: But before they make it

RACHEL: Before his fingers have the chance to grab

AARON: To wrap around the skin

EVIE: Finn pulls a hand out of his pocket

RACHEL: And quick as anything

AARON: He punches Gary's fat spongy stomach

EVIE: And instantly,

RACHEL: We immediately see it

AARON: Finn's hand.

RACHEL: Just fingers.

EVIE: Just a fist.

Just an empty fist.

They look at each other in sheer relief.

AARON: It's the silence

That cuts through you

RACHEL: As if everyone knew

EVIE: As if they're all holding their breath

RACHEL: What could have happened

EVIE: What very nearly did happen.

AARON: Even when the teachers run over

There's no sound

RACHEL: Just mouthed sentences

Just empty words

EVIE: One teacher leads them both away

AARON: For fighting

EVIE: Just

For fighting.

Pause.

RACHEL: And we see Farrah on the other side of the field

AARON: Not too close,

EVIE: But we see her in the distance

Watching her brother

RACHEL: Watching Finn and Gary

Walking inside

EVIE: She's like a beacon

Standing there in that jacket.

AARON: In Finn's jacket.

EVIE: You could spot her in a sandstorm.

END OF PLAY.

Salamander Street

**Teachers – if you are interested in buying a set of texts
for your class please email info@salamanderstreet.com
– we would be happy to discuss discounts and keep you up
to date with our latest publications and study guides.**

Follow us on Twitter or Facebook or visit our website
for the latest news.

www.ingramcontent.com/pod-product-compliance
Lightning Source LLC
Jackson TN
JSHW010854211224
75817JS00005B/132